A Barrel of Dried Leaves

Allan Cameron

A barrel not of laughs but of contortions, confusions
and the occasional dry chortle – and of metre adorned
with irregular, sometimes internal rhymes, assonances,
alliterations, awkwardnesses and other such trickery
unfashionable to the current academic ear, and not a
murmur of the poet's inner angst, failed loves or fortitude

Vagabond Voices
Glasgow

Published on 19 October 2016 by
Vagabond Voices Publishing Ltd.,
Glasgow,
Scotland.

ISBN: 978-1-908251-64-0

Printed and bound in Poland

Cover design and illustrations by Mark Mechan

Typeset by Park Productions

The author acknowledges subsidy from Creative Scotland
towards the writing of this book

For further information on Vagabond Voices, see the website,
www.vagabondvoices.co.uk

For Margaret

Contents

Preface

This collection is in many ways a continuation of my first, *Presbyopia*, which was published in 2009, but is more heterogeneous. This is strange because the earlier work was written over many years, in many different places, under more varying influences and even in two languages. *A Barrel of Dried Leaves* contains several poems that break with my own aesthetics, in particular "Sitting Ducks" (p. 47) which has an ugly metre. I have no idea where it came from, though the limerick and the nineteenth-century nonsense poem are clearly there. The intention was to use a disconcertingly childish tone to evoke cruelty and intolerance as a childish game. It also suggests that both perpetrators and victims are unable to behave differently, with only the ill-fated and conscience-stricken neighbour able to decide his fate. This is not something I believe and it was written not only outside my style but also outside my ideas (which are however always subject to powerful doubts). Yet I have no qualms about including it as, in spite of its ugliness, I think that it's one of my best.

In short, this poetry is stylistically more eclectic throughout the collection, though I purposefully placed "Sitting Ducks" immediately after "Aimless myopic prose with bits knocked out ...", the parody of a poem I heard on the radio that represented all I find tiresome about some modern poetry. Parody is different; it's an attempt to imitate someone else's aesthetic in order to undermine it.

Poems that exactly catch the essence of my own aesthetic are "Edgy Is Forgotten Now" (p. 4), "The Man with Soul So Dead" (p. 5), "The Little Language" (p. 8), "Where the Beauty, Where the Hope" (p. 42) and, clearly demonstrating the influence of Montale, "Scientific Progress" (p. 44). These are also fiercely presbyopic (as defined in the long introduction to *Presbyopia*), and express ideas.[1] "The Little Language" is about English and a plea not to exaggerate in changing our language because language is a bridge between generations. Too much change and communications break down.[2] Abstract ideas can be expressed beautifully and succinctly in poetry. Whether or not I succeed is not the point. We should return to it, and perhaps someone will come behind me and do it better.

An innovation in this collection, at least for me, is the presence of what I call portraits: "The String behind the Salt Crystals" (p. 18), "An Old Man Shuffles and Borbots" (p. 21), "A Momentary Meeting" (p. 22), "The Clever Man" (p. 24), "The Rich Man in His Castle" (p. 28) and others. These are rarely portraits of real people, and one exception is "The Clever Man" which was inspired by Wolfgang Schauble who insanely humiliated the Greek nation. Originally this was explicit in the title and a note below the poem, but with the passing of the months I fail to see why him and not others (and some gruesome politicians have come to prominence in the intervening period – not least in Britain). I prefer the positive note of "A Momentary Meeting", whose bright rhythm and rhyming scheme portray a lively woman who lives generously and within the moment. Such people are condemned with the expression, "Sufficient unto the day is the evil thereof", but they are the free spirits who bring light

---

1 In brief, the "presbyopic" poets focus on what is distant from them (ideas, abstractions, public discourse), and "myopic" poets (the self, poet's emotions or those who are close to the poet). For the record, I'm not saying the first are always good and the second always bad. And of course, there are plenty of hybrid poems.

2 I have a neck saying this, given that in this collection I invent the verb "to borbot" (a calque on *borbottare*) and means to mutter a little more loudly than "mutter" suggests in English.

to our lives or at the very least bring no threat of harm, as do so many more controlled and controlling people. I imagined my subject as a woman, but having glanced at the poem again, I see that her sex is never mentioned. So be it; she's a type who is possibly equally common in either sex.

My two Italian lessons were fun to write, and I hope that they're fun to read or hear, and do not appear to be tiresome, even shameless erudition. They're principally divertisse-ments, but the first, "Italian Lesson on Viticulture", suggests that meanings and their absences in languages affect the way we see the world, and "Italian Lesson in Anatomy" suggests that humans are very like animals, but also very different – and reiterates the question of language.

Lastly there are the narrative poems, "The Politburo in the Sky" (p. 13), "The Mystic" (p. 34), and *"This"* (p. 52). These I am passionate about, and they're never written in a single sitting, though normally in two or three days. The exception is "The Politburo in the Sky", whose first eight lines were written on a scrap of paper and lived precariously in the muddle of my desk. It was eventually excavated and I immediately knew what to do with it. Much later I used those first eight lines again to create very quickly an entry for the Thomas Gray Poetry Competition, hence a few ref-erences to the elegy in the poem, "Nature Looks Beat" (p. 31). The result is acceptable given the time pressures, and I include it to show how that start could have gone in different directions. The pleasant woman who advised me wondered if we still read English poets in Scotland, a sad reflections of how some English newspapers grossly misrepresented the independence referendum.

Allan Cameron, 14 June 2016

A Barrel of Dried Leaves

Freedom – I

Freedom, corroded word,
who could sing its anthem now?
Who could name the essence
of its deflated self?
And who, raising some banner high,
must not suppress desire to laugh
at so much hopeless hope,
and cannot but see in their own forceful acts
a parody of past.

Edgy Is Forgotten Now

The ribboned city roars its dull cacophony
of motor and of light.
Where's the scream, the yell, the hurts?
Where's the chatter that subverts or cracks
its hardened soul with wit?
Where's the love that conquers in defeat,
and where the honest smile that lights the way
to dauntless triggers of desire and mannered kindness
where fellow beings meet?

There are no actions, just transactions;
art is creative industry and books,
paintings, songs mere products to be sold –
to monetise, get the language right!
But have you seen the figures for the GDP
creative industry creates?
It has a purpose now it never had before;
it makes money move around, not ideas,
and thus is grounded in the real world of stuff.

Everything is learnt at school,
lawyered, sanitised and processed
not by experience and divergent whims,
but by the spec, the hardened rule,
the single, global textbook on it all –
best practice it is called. It changes
as the accountant, one eye on the market,
the other on new income streams, dictates.
Change doesn't change; it merely disrupts
and offers new business opportunities
to the rich. Ah! make a song of that.
Edgy is forgotten now, as is common chat.

The Man with Soul So Dead[*]

The man who could not say,
"This is my own, my native land,"
breathed freely
steadied his ambiguous frame
unframed by borders clearly drawn
and stamped with bureaucrats' approval.

"Stand free," he muttered to the wind
of changes marshalled by true soulless men.
"Count humans not compatriots," he cried,
dumbfounded by the stats for passported types
of human being,
which excluded others, luckless and unstamped.
"Starts here the road to unseen chances
of a different life beyond the market and the nation
as a myth to keep the nation down."

All men are one as are all nations,
and free them both by making countries
creative cooperatives not of kin
but of people who have drifted in
and learnt to live with open minds:
"This is my nation now I'm here,
until I move, but I hold dear
the whole – the rocks, the earth, the endless sand,
the planet whose pliant, pleasant land
is mine and yours and all we *should* call native."

---

[*] The poem is a response to Scott's more traditional nationalism suggested by the first three lines of one of his poems: "Breathes there the man with soul so dead,/ Who never to himself hath said,/This is my own, my native land."

Geopolitics

When spring is come and first I take
the pleasant lonely tread
along a mile or two of coast
to where the trawler bled
that lymph of engine oil and tar
on rocks that tore with slimy spikes
and left that dead machine to spread
its metal entrails on the bed
of seaweeds and of sand,

I think of how the fear and will to live
quickened the instincts of those who fled
the hard, well-fashioned anatomy of steel,
and furied as they did. Did ever so much happen
on that speck of land? – that is land only just;
its blackened symmetries barely outcrop
the well-ebbed sea; its unknown quantities –
an inner space, its canyons grander
for being conjured within my head.
The seamen lived, the vessel died,
the moment passed, the affected spread
on different paths of sea and ships,
and all that worthless, ill-focused frontier
of land and sea remembered for the fury
of a lonely moment in the place
where nothing happened to occur but once.

The sweet conjunction of salted scum,
blackened rock and sodden earth
held its little history dear – a tale
of skirmish on the embattled borders
between empire of the land
and empire of the sea.

The Little Language

Who made the sounds that echo in the chambers
of our minds, if not collective genius
and genial discoursing of generations past?
Let me make a plea then
for this little language that has become too strong.
You say it must evolve and sculpt new voices
fitting to the virtues and vices of our times,
and how right you are.

But leave that hammer down! Don't touch
the key the JCB responds to at a turn.
You don't open up and make free
our parlance when you shatter all the filigree
that holds the nuance and the psalm
together in a weave of words
rooted in the past.

Change of course, or else we die,
but do not play iconoclast
and leave the dead for dead.
In language all is upside down,
and forward is reverse.
That wall you see is paper thin –
a construct of our minds;
that wall you're knocking down
with grand, heroic hammer blows
builds another one of stone,
that tall it rives us from voices
deceased but not till now
departed from our minds.

Lesson in Italian Viticulture

Uva should have the bitter taste of life
and not the sweet,
should hold   the heat of the sun
and linger on the tongue,
when autumn mildly warms
the firm-fleshed fruit clinging to the stalk
in comfort and in company
of the *grappolo*,*
the whole that has no singular
in the language of its collective realm.
Uva translates the grape
eaten in colder clime.

---

* In Italian, *Uva* is a collective noun for grapes, and a grape is a *chicco d'uva* and
a bunch of grapes is a *grappolo d'uva*.

The Good Knight and His Spin Doctor

Crowne Plaza played its weary tune,
a child's melody of warbled greys
a jingle that mirrored Glasgow's mottled sky,
a hymn to uniformity of place and time,
a song that kills all song, and leaves us cold
to crush the leaves the fall blew in.

A soulless place in which to trudge,
the Ministry of Truth across the Clyde,
as square as Crowne is tall, glints
its own message of steel and glass.
What a pair, Quixote and Panza
in their stationary quest to rule all time,
and keep us within their thrall.

And the Clyde flows on,
one of the world's small arteries,
carrying the clamour of yesteryears
and vibrant uncertainties of years to come.
On a fledgling tree, leased no doubt
by a Brussels firm who never knew the sapling
nor the man who planted roots of its frail frame,
a bird breaks the desert stillness of the day
with a flutter of wings and then it calls,
as calls the grumble of traffic on Kingston Bridge,
heavy with the many moments of the many
as they rush to important appointments
soon forgotten in the flow of feelings
always revived by busyness that numbs.

The Politburo in the Sky

Nature looks beat, and who,
calling into the night, will plead
its cause before the politbure of good and bad,
consisting, it's said, of God and entourage of holy souls
deeply concerned with their own inner grace,
and the devil's court of outraged greed,
grinning entrepreneur'al energy at the other side.
And will he be heard?

Then came a man of languid heart,
who sixty years had lain in death,
diseased but stubborn in his quest to claim
his rightful share of health and vibrant life.
"Living truth," he whispered to the dark,
the dark recesses of his mind poisoned by his loss,
"You gave me this, this half share of life,
and asked that I be sated by a niggard gift."

"That God gifts His gifts in unequal measure,
and that we let the numbered balls roll
randomly to cast each human fate is, I fear,
just part of the game," one saint said whilst
he enamelled his nails with a most perfect red,
"You must accept the hand you're dealt, you know.
It's no use lamenting your allotted place,"
he grinned and waved his little lacquered brush.
"It is too bad, I fully comprehend."

A devil, louche with measured ease, chewed his claw
as though it were a sugared plum, and raised a lazy brow
heavy with disdain: "To pity self is to make me sick.
We damned and damaged souls have got it good
as very bad can only get better. Die, and we will warm you up.
New Labour stole our anthem, and you'll hear nothing else."

"And justice?" said the little man.
Oh how they laughed, saints and devils both,
and how they clapped their thighs, the saints
more rambunctious, the devils more aloof.

"Let me be clear," opined the chair,
a man of girth whose opulence declared
his status as the depute to the Demiurge
of all that is. "Justice reigns
and should never be appealed.
Justice is the will and whim of His almighty force.
What is is good, and what is not
should never be desired.
His competence is unbounded
and any sickened soul who questions it
is promptly damned to everlasting hell."

The fop, whose silkened threads, lacquered hands
and hair well-coiffured and set spoke clearly
of his saintly soul well-beloved of God,
could not hold in check his dreary voice
deepened by dull certitudes of those who are secure:
"The evil and the good in each one of them
should be allocated with a view to all
the good and evil spread around and held collective
to the human soul and institutions."
Up *spracht* the angel cloaked in black and staring

dark-eyed, fiercely through his *pince-nez à la* Trotsky
that underscored his intellect fine and broad
but prone to rigor mortis and italics in his speech.
"My bourgeois colleague, noted decadent and leech
excuses all by his pragmatic joyless joy of living
just for pleasure!" he barked with Lutheran precision.
"Too sweet of you," the sainted dandy dignified
his answer with a smile concealing an incision
to the Trotsky's pretension to moral ascendancy,
"but they," he swept his arm to indicate amorphous mass,
humanity by metric ton, "live in the real world
we have imagined and decreed, and to ignore evil
is to engender more. They must live with evil
and inflict with evil deeds the lesser evil
we all desire."

Glumly sat the satans in surprise, outflanked
in evil where their most cogent discourse barely stirred.
"Enough," said Sugared Plum, pissed-off,
and prickly was his default state,
"you work with lies and cunning,
clever talk that has neither head nor tail;
we work with claw" (he held it high)
"and sword, and sharpened bits,
and guns of every shape and size
and rockets, smart and not,
and hunger, siege and mustard gas,
our prize the atom bomb."

His comrade rose, strapping but not prolix
in his wording of what was dearest
to his heart:
"Hypocrites, we temper our greed
with the courage of our acts.

We do not whimper, simper or complain.
He cast us down, but still we fight.
We are who we are
and would not be other than ourselves
with honest passion for power
fairly won with bloodied hands."
And down he sat, the picture
of an outraged soul.

"But where is God?" the sick man said.
"You hold His court without Him."
"When did He come last?" the chairman mused,
perplexed and racking the corners
of his flaccid brain, wearied by the task.
"Who does recall? God muddles space and time."
"Not punctual, I would say," the dandy played his part.
"God has faith in us. Our acts he does ordain,"
the Trotsky added, "the protocol is complex
for his visits to the court. It would not do
to have Him mess with daily management
of life and death, good and bad,
and counting out the dead.
He leaves all that to us!"

"Better a month with sickened soul and ailing body
in human concourse, mixed and full of strains,
than lingering and over-rehearsed eternity
in company of diabolic saints and rabid fools
unsated by a drive to hurt, where courage
is mere bluster and bombast – last inklings
of a defeated crew," said the weak man still in mortal flesh,
arraigned before the light and dark; "where is the new,
when time has no border to make it real?
Where is our God? He is not here to elucidate,

to make it clear why afterlife is conflicted too,
and dull, disjointed, not engaged, unchallenged
in this timeless sphere." "He'll not come for you,
you speck of life that hardly glowed; He is for us,
the bureaucrats and businessmen of His eternal
market of our dreams; He never mixes with the erks,"
said the dandy joyful in the perquisites of power.
"He is not here, I'm certain now," the weak man brightened up,
"He does not live in this empyrean realm at all,
it was not Satan's fall but His. Escaping mannered mirth
and unhurried hate, He came to us ephemera you burden
with your wants. He is in us, He is on earth."

The String behind the Salt Crystals
or
Art and Intellect Lost to Power

You

spoke loudly when first we came
to know each other's hearts.

You

desired above all else the fame
of being a woman of many parts.

You

demanded and commanded my respect
and instilled in me a faith in

you.

Don't get me wrong; I recollect
I loved your song, your play thing.

You

detested plainness in other lives
and thought you rose to higher plane.

You

scoffed at her who strives
through life while keeping sane.

You

claimed the heights of intellect and art
but they caught you in middle-class mores
and taught you to love approval,
not removal from the self
which alone allows creative acts
founded on human justice,
not selective facts.

Freedom – II

The animal, saddened by abstractions
it invented in loquacious ecstasy,
sold the soul they generated
for an embrace of baubles
that would suck the planet dry.

The animal, fattened by affluence
and poisoned by the effluence of affluence
could no longer understand the abstractions
gifted by loquacity, now withered,
now words exploited to obfuscate
and not illuminate the darkened lonely lane
that leads to freedom from insane
desires to consume the unnecessary
and control the uncontrollable.

An Old Man Shuffles and Borbots

"Who would fancy me –
old man who sadly shuffles
and borbots bilious regrets?"
His past, a solid crag or silted river –
he does not know – is never wholly there,
but is. With it he is alone,
but it's company, of a kind.
Where's the touch, the yearning grasp,
the hope of moments yet to come,
and dialogues to make?
Its hollow song – the only siren left –
denotes its hollow will to live.
When he dies, so will it –
companions of a kind.
But does it live or hold from life
that last glimmer of being, being sensual
in a feeling world of beings lost in space,
still with senses muffled by the coming dark,
but senses nonetheless?

A Momentary Meeting

Tell me not the god you plunder
for your thoughts, desires and wonder!
Tell me not the seeds you scatter
vainly hoping to define the matter
future brings with stealth and flatter...ry!
Tell me not the dreams that move you,
soothe you with their promise to you
of love and wealth that can approve you
for a life of calm and ease.
Tell me now what creature are you,
who struggles so and stares so far you
hardly notice what you do do.
You smile and laugh and lift us to you,
enigma, humane hustling being,
lost in life and therefore seeing
all there is within this moment fleeing.

The Poet Spoke

There was a truth in what she said;
some words so sweet they made me cry
with my delight in how
I nearly understood their scope,
their draw, their charm, their perfect balance,
and how well they carried it,
that truth, I mean.
Elusive, barely sketched,
it shimmered in my mind, and grew;
a warmth so cool
my fingers felt the coarse irony
and the smooth restraint
she mastered with a will
to please, to teach, to startle
and, above all, to confound.

The Clever Man
or
An Epitaph for a German finance minister who killed the E.U. dead and told the Demos what to do

He was a clever man, but very cold.
He knew it all, but never knew
what it was not to know the firmness of his place.

He was a clever man, but very bold.
He knew it all, but never knew
what it was to fear his fall from grace.

He was a clever man, but never starved.
He knew it all, but never knew
what it was to go without a meal.

He was a clever man, but never strayed.
He knew it all, but never knew
what it was not to feel …
the whispers of another's dreams.

He never knew where what is
diverges from what seems.

Time and My Wife

I have wasted many things
and many things have taught me why
I wasted all these years. Life!
Ambition too came snaking through the grass,
pleasure thickened lazy days
and busy times dried out the human humours
of my heart. I spoke and held too keenly
to my thoughts. I loved not women real
in heart and mind, but constructs of what
I wanted them to be. I gave, but wanted back
my gift with interest on account.
I studied, foolish in my wish to be the best at something
no one values any more.

And then you came and held me strong;
led me out and took me to the vantage
of my faults. The pleasure is in the act itself:
the giving, loving, feeling, seeing the tight
compactness of this lonely, cluttered world
in which a perfect sun rises on Cox's Beach
and wintry blasts do scour the Arctic wastes.
Every life is a voyage between the one and the other.
At the beach, you dug your hands deep and laughed apace
with all the brightness of your soul, and sand like snow
weeping fell and carried in the wind.

Lesson in Italian Anatomy

Bones are *ossa* when they human are,
but *ossi* when products of fauna,
our coeval ancestors
our living ghosts articulated
by a common frame.
Ossa are a humanistic survival
of the plural neuter in the Latin tongue,
eccentric discrimination
between the speechless
and the speechifiers
on this crowded ball in space.
And *membra*,
limbs to live with through our shared decay
and luxuriant revival
of all that lives.

Only the Lonely Have a Soul

He came, short man with thinning hair
and eyes upturned seeking assurance
from the enigma of your face,
and quickly turning down, evading your collected self,
and then he spoke.

You smiled benignly, conscious of your space,
and the fragile nature of your cultured soul,
and his words spilled and quickened
as he felt their strength,
as though relearning skills forgotten in the slide of time,
and you shifted weight to show
your patience was not thick.
You nodded slyly, as what he said
was of some worth,
and could be stored for future use.

And then he stopped, plugged by quizzical disdain
you offered with generous aplomb.
"It has been good," he said at last,
squeezing your hand too hard,
to meet with one like you,
an honour I must heed
and not exceed in draining off your time."

The Rich Man in His Castle

There comes no call nor bride of fear
to stir his mind with concepts new
or doubts antique.
He stirs instead his massive frame,
a synecdoche,
a gross grotesque,
a caricature not of capitalism
but of what it has become.
A part of the whole, which his bulk
describes with eloquent, dull directness.

He stands and carries all the mass that feeds
on what he cannot comprehend,
and contains not just fat, bone and muscle too
to prop exorbitant weight,
but also greed.
He moves in space but not in thought,
and the calorific counter speeds.
He speaks and calls in all his wants,
his entitlement to men, women
and boys,
they're all for sale
somewhere in the meanders
of the planetary slum,
and even close to home
when urges urge.

His flattened face has lifeless eyes
and the beard, a speckled scum,
denotes that one thing grows
under that epidermis sated now,
but not for long.
His substance is Saville-Rowed
and well-adorned with Gucci,
Armani and a Rolex watch.
His buttered flab is full
of empty cells of plenitude,
leaking sweat of energy unused.

The Cat That Unwittingly Inspires ...

The feline, oblivious to the world,
apparently,
snobbed me with a turn of her head
and a tremble of her whiskers,
an Anglicisation of an Italian Anglicism;
clever for a cat who knows no grammar
or etymology
or words indeed,
and yet it has ...
(you'll note how I put in that "it"
to put it in its place, that cat)
... a better sense of where it's placed
within this world
than do I,
whose feelings spin a verbal thread
to display nature's superabundance,
its exuberant excess
like peacock feathers in the sun.
There's pleasure in that –
my disarray, a little fun –
for which I thank the cat.

Nature Looks Beat

Nature looks beat, and who,
calling into the night, will plead
its cause before the politbure of good and bad,
consisting, it's said, of God and entourage of holy souls
deeply concerned with their own inner grace,
and the devil's court of outraged greed,
grinning entrepreneur'al energy at the other side.
And will she be heard?

A woman came, and kicked the purer earth
that lay around half-buried headstones
where the paths of glory grandly were declared,
and she, more wary now the housing schemes
were marching close and trimming out the sky,
stood firm and raised the coolness of her voice
to meet the silent counsel of the planet's needs,
"Where is the cleanness of our hearts, and where your words?"
she asked, "now poison outwith this yard silences the birds.

"Where death has found its home, a little life survives;
beyond extend the schemes and endless replica'd prairie
filled with phosphates of our greeds that sow
seeds of destruction for our green planet
whose grave but graveless death we will not know."

Riflusso[*]

All of the words the day had sprung
the night has buried now.
Now do the hopes we cherished then
seem dark and shameful to our weaker sort
and those who took the ride.

From high upon our greatest chance,
the structures of our hierarking chiefs,
whose loyalty to equal lives was largely
founded on their grand usage of the state
and the comfort of their over-equal fate,
made war and weapons quite grotesque
and not inclined to free mankind –
but to destroy it.

---

[*] *Riflusso*: a return to conservative thinking; disengagement with politics

The Mystic

I died and having died
could no more feel the touch of life
but lived, and living, moved
within a shell, which hollowed out,
contains a wealth of emptied thoughts
that settle, like dried leaves, lining
the bottom of my soul, sediment
of a life that's passed away.

My brother fights with hatred in his heart.
Because he fights, he lives and hopes.
Because he hopes, he builds
a future in this head.
Because he builds, he feels his body
move within a world to which he still belongs.

The foreign soldiers came and fought
a folly of a war.
They knew how to be killed and killed
in turn. They shone in our sun
and smelt of milk and acrid tears.
The fears they brought never left with them,
but clung like mist to hills and mountain roads,
and dampened our dry hearts
and dulled the brightness of our songs
the students later took.

And took for good; their rigid rules –
some vain hope of order where war
decreed the chaos of our lives.
The order clashed with other orders
better ordered, better armed and
driven by some rapacious force.

Then there was the wedding feast;
a column of our cars was snaking through
the hamlets, orchards, arid tracts
of this, our Afghan land.
And yes, the joy, the smiling crowds,
the waving wedding guests, gleeful
on the back of trucks, their open hearts,
their loving talk, the child's excited chatter,
enveloped in a thin, translucent cloud of dust.

Fierce, so fierce, the horror came,
the airplane stumbled in our skies
and cast its bombs like seeds of death,
and swooped and swung like the groom's mother
who moving in a trance does dance and show
her bitter jubilation.
Something starts and something ends.
Something changes now forever.

And so did I. I died when the moment died,
and quickly such a crop of bloodied bodies
stretched in the thicker dust of wailing sorrow.
Life died in me, but my hollow corpse
moves on, or stills itself in huddled form
beside the pleasant river.
Long hours I spend in empty thought,
while all around they argue, scream
and laugh again, bold builders
of their future selves. They mix
with foreign lords and my brother's
band of fighters – each the image of their foe.

Like a diseased tree whose healthy bark
conceals its vacant trunk that stays erect
and dismally awaits the blessed wind that'll fell it,
I cross-legged sit and nothing stirs
the desiccated leaves of thought.
They call me mad for looking on
the madness of their world in silence.

Life's a Bitch
(or The Deist's God Goes Walking in a Back Lane)

The father, silent in his thoughts, guided
the pushchair down a darkened lane.
The child, glum but with no signs of pain,
unprovoked did scream an anguished scream
that parted from the heart, the centre
of his being. Red eyes, red face, red hair:
red fury scolded sky and all
the hapless clutter of that narrow lane,
where human life was only known
by its detritus. Father continued
unconcerned, unseeing of the fragile load
that life unloaded on his eternal tread.
He judged but did not intervene.

Poets and Poetry Writers

Being a poet is no fun:
always staring pensively
at a slightly disappointing distant horizon
keeping silent to acquire an air of hauteur
and blessed detachment,
being poetic to everyone
including yourself,
being overwhelmed by your exceptionalism,
a burden to be borne with courage.

Writing poetry is fun,
just as the ad for the creative writing course promised
(and you never went),
jotting down ideas that don't always work,
waking up in the night with six lines fully formed,
and you can still natter in aimless unformed sentences,
slurp your soup,
laugh at your unaesthetic self,
admit that you never read *The Faerie Queene*
or *The Wasteland*,
and not move with the pack,
except when writing about poetry.

The Poverty of Wealth

"How poor you are, my gilded friend,"
I said and watched his wrinkled face.
"I?" he laughed and heaved his chest
with grandeur suited to his sharpened state.
"I have a corporation listed on the bourse,
a yacht whose cabinets are filled with drink
to keep my retinue tight within the joyless joy
the sycophant encounters while securing
comfort for his future days living in my shadow.
I have a house so large, I cannot know
the number of its rooms, the meanders
of its patronage to souls deflated by my power.
I am a king whose subjects do not know my name;
I little care for vassalage from those so low
they cannot see the strings I pull to make them move
their hollow carcasses across their broken dreams.
You call me poor, you ragged man who beckons
with the arrogance of thought. Clear my path
or I shall crush you like the worm you are."
"A sorry state is yours indeed," I sympathised
with all my heart. "What you call carcasses
are full of hope and gentle kindness
that lives forever in the human soul.
A carcass passive like a fallen leaf told one
such as you to cast away his riches
and then to follow. They crushed him
as the worm they reckoned him to be,
and then their children made him king of kings,
who pronounces on all their hidden wants
and justifies their power. His real children
are the poor, who hold eternal riches
in their sagging arms. His real children

are the abused whose names are dragged
through streams of mud. His real children
are the dispossessed whose voices
are not heard. And yet what riches
they encounter on their heavy trudge
through life: their loves, their likes, their losses
all come carrying them to the greenness of their death,
unlike yours, that lonely thing that divides you
from the barren fertility of wealth."
"Away you madman. I'll not touch the contagion
of your thought. I'll not whip the fool, though
you deserve it well," he seethed.
"I am a shadow of your own fear," I answered him again,
"and similar fools will come as the sunlight
plays on each green budding leaf. I am each second
of your corroded brain. Each second that cries
for freedom from the stuff that in making stuff is fecund."

Where the Beauty, Where the Hope

A young man walked his dog,
and his bravado too.
Behind, modern builds of square and Lego look
grouped their sadness in a lot
of awkward silence
at their lifeless dress.
He swung the stick that held a ball,
well-chewed no doubt, and off it went,
the dog in chase. Predictable
as the starting of that sullen day.

The parkland's paths he held within his head,
and well he knew that none
could lead him from the drudge his life'd become.
Beyond, what else would be there but strangers
staring in disbelief at the ilk of conformity
he'd take with him? More dull hillocks,
shocks of weeds, and rivers running dark
and loaded with the discards of consumer life.

Where the beauty, where the hope?

There's a Stench of the Thirties

Long before the killing came,
they showed their yellow teeth,
and danced the paranoid
with verve and nifty feet.
"Send Johnny back," they sentenced
with the mien of a judge,
"He's after jobs, the lazy lout,
and binges benefits he senses
with that olfactive miracle
he calls his snout.
He ogles OUR women, the saucy git,
and if we were men, we'd keep him out.
If we were men, we'd stand up true
and, like our forbears who went everywhere,
we'd tell Johnny Foreigner what he's got to do."

Scientific Progress

The words that are not said,
but shouted from the roofs
are hollowed out, and stripped
of sense and sound that carries
doubt and complex quirks of knowing not
the whys and wherefores of the beauties
of this world...

The sea loch's vast, and paints a mottled blue
before my eyes.
Beyond, a strip of brownish flatland
catches a patch of brightness
the clouds have failed to grasp.
Below, near to the rocks, a man –
a darkened silhouette – busies in the wind,
as does his jacket – blue, I think.
The purpose of his rushing back and forth
eludes me, as do many things.

The kitchen clock is running late
but beats the rhythm of our time
no less. A half hour passes and still
he's running left and right. He has a rope!
I've grown my knowledge base! And then,
he's gone and took those busied moments
he'd displayed.
In the stillness of the quiet field below
a grey goose waddles slow and sure
about the business of eating grass.
The empty washing line jerks rhythmic,
pointless, endless in the breeze. The clouds
closed off the light illumining

the drab thread of a Highland town.
All has darkened, and in that dull light,
my not knowing lifts my heart,
excites my sense of living
in this most intoxicating point in space.

Sitting Ducks
or Predestined Objects

Why must we muddle minds of sitting ducks
along our garden wall?
We give them candy as a bate,
we give them dollars and dimes
to imprice them to dance the cukuroo
which tickles and chimes with our fancygate.
"Quack quack," they eguterate;
it's all that they can do.

Our neighbour said we shouldn't
tease the avians so;
it wasn't in their nature
to wangle in the glow.
They have a heart, but couldn't
find the will to negate your
devious adfartments and cunning toldyouso.

No one likes a smart arse.
No one likes a snob,
so we lifted up a cudgel
and struck him round the head,
nor were we slightly bothered
when he fell down slightly dead.

In answer to my question,
I really couldn't say;
I think it's cos we have no
other way to play.

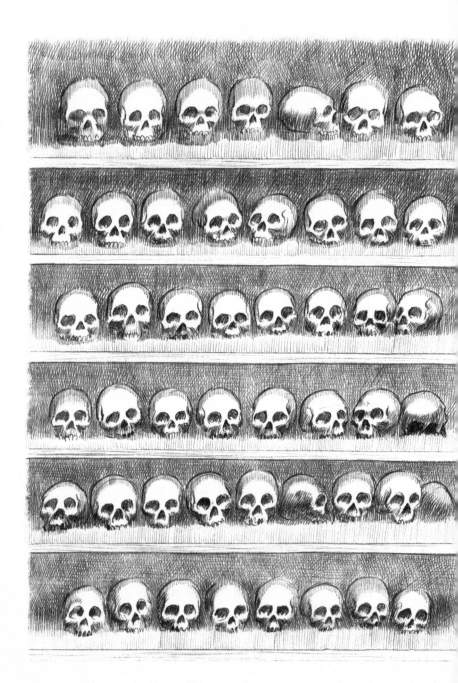

On Seeing a Photo of Victims' Skulls from the Cambodian Genocide

The grinning teeth and vacant stares, they have no purpose,
nor do their daily cares sift and shake the fibre of their bones.
Which was the slender lad whose passions stalked a female frame
he could not banish from his thoughts? Where is the girl
who sang so sweet, her feelings echoed in her schoolmates' heads?
The brooding teacher vanquished by the failure of her years,
the greedy trader whose mind just counts the movements
of his wealth, the sullen housewife once instructed in French
and foreign ways, the brawny warehouse worker who seldom sought
to cause offence or darken others' days, they all vacated what was
theirs
and hastened off or were. They left these shells, indictments of a
crime so foul,
it weighs upon the human mind and questions who we are.

I see these skulls so neatly ordered on their shelves like books or pans
or useful things – they're not. Read them if you can, I cannot find
the syntax of their hollow laugh; they have one letter, that is all,
and look alike: ghastly fruits grown in the garden of our most
gruesome thoughts.
To stare at their staring orbs is to intrude on others' holy grief
and to turn away is turning from what should never be forgot,
into oblivion's unfeeling want of nothing but the comfort of the self,
blinder than these dear blinded and hurted discards of souls
whose silence is their loudest roar.

Aimless myopic prose with bits knocked out gets you into the echo chamber

Here we are in our small, smug minds
happy to let the first things that come into them
leap gamely on to the paper and on the air:
BBC 2, Radio 4, Radio 4, BBC 2.
There's a big bouncy world out there, harbours,
the seven seas, Fortnum and Mason, the Eiffel Tower.
We could be at Henley, but actually we're here,
happy to let genteel minds wander and preach power
to complacent ears.

The Buriganga

Wide, wide and sturdy the river ran the Bengal plain
It swelled a murky blue and slunk along
in its steady thoughtful way.

The country boats, still heavy lifters of the delta trade,
moved with purpose under a gentle wind that played
upon the ruffles of a timeless calm of the soul.

Steamers paddled as they always had
since they left Dumbarton near a century before,
their huge pistons fed by near naked stokers
in a tiny circle of earthly hell,
five categories of human being
and ticket price upon their decks,
some herded into pens, some waited on at dinner.
A smaller vessel, faster too,
carried tipsy white folk on a jaunt,
who waved at a world busy in its slow reflection,
while they were busy having fun.
Gently, gently the steamers' muscles flexed
and manoeuvred through the crowd,
the anarchic, nautical multiculturalism of the river-lake.

This

Conscience and its
failures.

To *this* and all the sadness of this world
I write these words of happy oblivion
desired and almost gained! I felt
and feared that at some future date
I would feel no more.
No more hear the cries of pain that sear the night
and invade my dreams. But then I felt and always feared
that I would never cease to feel those pointless wounds
that never brought a balm to those who scream
and doubtless suffer out of sight.

Memory and the
struggle to retain it.
We live in history but
cannot see it. Our will
is feeble but essential in
its feebleness

This is a struggle to retain – to re-evoke those moments
of the past that could slip away like leaves scattered by a
gust
or simply rotting where they lie,
losing all the colours they displayed on the branch
or brightened and nuanced during early stages
of their desiccation.
Memories take on bright golds, yellows and reddish
browns
burnished by their retelling. And then they too rot or
carry
far off in rushing time so they can come back blasting
into our brains heavy with new meanings. These joys
and bitter blows lift or shatter hopes and tell us truths
of what *this* is – the crazy thing we all know well
and yet cannot define.

I try to recall what I witnessed
standing safely at a hotel window,
while the smallest cogs of history turned
and ground another people's hopes to dust,
as they always do.
I saw the crowd of sans-culottes, then full of faces
but faceless now the image fades –
a crowd of Bengalis in their lungis and singlets
marching by the million to the racetrack,
hemmed in on every side by soldiers
wielding batons lethargically, beating without passion,
without zest, because they had to.
And these same soldiers, Bengalis too, some months from then
would fight and die for a nation they would never see,
forgotten in history's unforgiving flood.

The image fades but not what I have learnt: there are
few wholly good or evil men, only individuals swept along,
now and then resisting – vainly – all the vicious power
of the amorphous flood.

*We live through the experience
of our senses*

This is to feel with all our senses sharpened by the will to be –
to be in the moment and forget
for once the weight of years to come or drawn behind –
that dragged us down or will.
This moment sweet – to lie within another's arms and feel
the smoothness of her skin, the involucre of her warm
and naked soul. This moment when the wind comes in
and bites the cheeks with unrelenting force –
nature that cohabits still this manufactured land.
This lunch when food plays long and vibrant
on our budding nerves and slips forgotten
into the abyss of our unending needs.

And how we shout and turn upon each other
with our cares, our thoughts, our strong beliefs
of all the things we cannot know with any certitude.
We fret and manipulate our words, wanting to win –
but what? And will they understand those words
in a century, in a decade's time or even in ten days from now?
We have the now. We stand in it and declare our truths.

Inferno here on earth.
Suffering teaches but
also destroys.

And now those vinous moments of the now are in the past
and mainly inhabit my memories of Italy, a land
where they know how to talk and did.
The flasks of wine, the grated cheese that smelt,
the oil so new it stung upon the tongue,
all those heady, heady words that melt within the brain and
touch those nerves that, for too long,
have not had anything to feel or grasp.

This hell, this hole: how many times do we return
to the darkness of the past?
This earthly hell is surely not followed by unearthly one.
This feeling trapped within the self,
a bag of nerves that jangle not just with our own pain,
but also with our compassion for others.
Our pain, if it does not break us, makes us strong
and therefore serves a purpose.
If ever you foolishly dwell on the pains of your past,
then take a look at the pompous prick
who pampered all his life now smugly observes
from his position of great or petty power
his secure kingdom of unappreciated delights
and honours granted for his acceptance
of the hierarchic chain into which he so snugly fits.

Such people at the slightest slight
react with anger or self-pity,
heedless that success merely locks the door
to the cell in which the self is caught,
and makes a prison of a tight abode.

This is also made of raptures, those moments of escape
when the mind concentrates on one thing
and distils its pleasure from some problematic
of a kind our passions can delight in.
A sport, a broke-down car, a mountain face, a place unknown,
a book, a canvas stabbed with paint,
these all suppress the self, throw wide the cell door and reveal
the limitless plain of ways and ways of doing,
seeing, moving, searching, calling, expressing
to others and to oneself the permutations
of how we can consume *this*, this elusive thing
we never notice until it is at risk.

The artist measured up his work with steady eyes
and critically calculated all those marks of paint:
the colours, contrast, composition,
brushwork, pose, poise, expression of the hurt,
pathos of the suffering saint –
a noose loosely fitted round his scraggy neck.
Then he leapt, large brush in hand
heavy with black paint.
And how he laboured with that destructive arm,
which spread a night across the surface of his work.
No dawn would resurrect the fearsome portrayal
of a martyred end. But still he paints a lonely figure

whose afflicted corpse-to-be stands free of ground,
of time, of pain perhaps,
levitated by the energy of sacrifice.
The hooded hangman's noose is gone,
so has the crowd that gleeful jostled
and stretched forward to enjoy the show.
The light of the heavens triumphant has been dulled,
so loneliness remains.

Microcosm and
macrocosm

This contains those civic moments
by which we measure out the passing years:
birth, pair-bonding of some kind, birth of children,
the repeating cycle of their *this*, and then death.
This, rather grandly, also posits such events
within the timeline history dictates:
"two years before the war", "just after the recession",
"when they landed on the moon".
This is how the micro- and the macrocosm should relate:
their unequal trajectories are not mechanic things –
the individual can rebel and should.
This belongs beyond oneself and beyond the triteness
of one's age and its conformist certitudes.

What this is. You
haven't guessed?

This is this little thing that seems so big,
this life we share, this tangle of shattered nerves,
this string of thoughts that lonely twist and turn,
fly up into the airless light where ideas are born
and the gods sing, or sink into the deep,
depressing water that presses on our lungs
and cruelly clears away all hope,
where drags us down the leaden weight

of that elusive thing we call the real.
Like all small things, this life's capable of endless variegations,
and the stack of stuff of which it's made
can be shuffled in so many ways.
In one backyard behind a block of flats,
a history of lives can be played out,
and more happens
in one small child's brain
than in several light-years of space.
This is a divine gift we have to please ourselves,
to please others and to waste, and of course regret.

When life's end comes, it's a book that's writ
and left unread. No chance to correct and polish here –
the pages are turning yellow.
It's a story randomly told and what it lacks and incoheres
is made up for in its tragicomic commerce of traducements
and prodigal human passions.